A. Lincoln

A COMMITMENT
TO HONOR

A COMMITMENT TO HONOR

A Unique Portrait of Abraham Lincoln in His Own Words

Compiled and Edited by

GORDON LEIDNER

RUTLEDGE HILL PRESS®

Nashville, Tennessee

A Thomas Nelson Company

Published in Nashville, Tennessee, by Rutledge Hill Press,® a Thomas Nelson Company, P.O. Box 141000, Nashville, Tennessee 37214.

Design by Gore Studios

Typography by Roger A. DeLiso, Rutledge Hill Press®

Library of Congress Cataloging-in-Publication Data
Lincoln, Abraham, 1809–1865.
   A commitment to honor : a unique portrait of Abraham Lincoln in his own words / compiled and edited by Gordon Leidner.
      p.   cm.
   ISBN 1-55853-786-4 (hc)
   1. Lincoln, Abraham, 1809–1865 Quotations.   2. Presidents—United States Quotations. 3. United States—Politics and government Quotations, Maxims, etc.   4. Conduct of life Quotations, maxims, etc.   I. Leidner, Gordon, 1954–   .   II. Title.
E457.99.L4   1999
973.7'092—dc21   99-38776
                                        CIP

Printed in the United States of America
   2 3 4 5 6 7 8 9—03 02 01

To Jean—

WITH LOVE

CONTENTS

Preface

Americans have been fascinated with Abraham Lincoln for more than a century. Our fascination with and respect for Lincoln is rooted in his legacy both as a preserver of the Union and as the Great Emancipator. We also esteem him as the embodiment of integrity, faith, generosity, and determination. He persevered and fought his way up to occupy the highest office of the land, doing so without benefit of wealth or formal education. We value his state papers, speeches, and letters as eloquent testimonies of statesmanship and striking character. Ever since Lincoln's death at the hands of an assassin, people have acknowledged that his life is an excellent example of what determination and industry can accomplish under democratic government.

My interest in Lincoln and the American Civil War began during my childhood. I grew up in southern Illinois, where Lincoln lore is integral to local history. In September 1858 my hometown of Greenville was honored with a visit by Abraham Lincoln in between his Great Debate appointments at Freeport and Jonesboro. Vandalia, a neighboring community, is home of the second state capitol and is where Lincoln began his political career as a state representative from Sangamon County. Vandalia has the added distinction of being the city where Lincoln first publicly declared the "injustice" of slavery.

My task in assembling this book of Lincoln quotations primarily was to wade through mountains of Lincoln material, distinguish the genuine from the proverbial, and then attempt to select the best of the best. The quotes herein are taken from the sources listed in the endnotes. I've occasionally made minor changes in punctuation in order to improve readability, but the original misspellings are for the most part left uncorrected.

Lincoln lived his life with a commitment to honor, and in this book the admirable qualities and virtues he embodied are examined in some detail and through his words. Included in each of the twelve chapters are observations of Lincoln by some of the people who knew him best, validating Lincoln's association with the discussed virtue. Think of this book as an inspirational and motivational guide on how to live life today, emulating the great qualities of perhaps our nation's greatest leader ever.

ABRAHAM LINCOLN BIOGRAPHY

Abraham Lincoln was born near Hodgenville, Kentucky, on February 12, 1809. He was raised by poor parents and had received less than a year of formal education by the time he turned twenty-one. He moved to New Salem, Illinois, in 1831 and continued his self-education there by borrowing books and teaching himself subjects such as grammar, history, mathematics, and law.

Outgoing and ambitious, Lincoln was anxious to make his mark in politics. He was elected one of Sangamon County's Whig representatives to the Illinois state legislature in 1834. Vocally anti-slavery, he served four consecutive terms as state legislator, during which time he was admitted to the Illinois bar. He soon became one of the most respected lawyers in the region, known particularly for his honesty and influential manner with juries.

In 1842 Lincoln married Mary Todd, a well-educated woman of a notable Kentucky family. They eventually had four sons, although only one survived to manhood.

Lincoln served a term in Congress from 1847 to 1849. He then went into semiretirement from politics in order to concentrate on his law practice. The Kansas-Nebraska Act of 1854, allowing for the introduction of slavery into the new territories, enticed Lincoln to again seek political office. He joined the Republican Party in 1856 and ran for the U.S. Senate in 1858, providing energetic moral argument against slavery in the Great Debates with Stephen A. Douglas.

Lincoln lost the senate race to Douglas but two years later, in 1860, was elected president. Subsequent to his election, eleven southern states declared their independence from the Union. Although Lincoln knew that slavery was the underlying cause of the war, he realized that to declare a war against slavery would result in many of the northern people's refusal to fight. When the South fired on Fort Sumter on April 12, 1860, Lincoln declared a war to preserve the Union and called the North to arms.

It was more than a year into the Civil War before Lincoln was finally able to add the elimination of slavery to the war's purposes. His Emancipation Proclamation, freeing the slaves of the rebelling southern states, took effect on January 1, 1863. Subsequent Union victories at Gettysburg, Vicksburg, and Chattanooga soon had the southern armies permanently on the defensive. Lincoln was reelected president in November 1864.

Lincoln's second inaugural address, delivered less than six weeks before his assassination, eloquently summed up his beliefs: that the underlying cause of the war had been slavery; the war was God's punishment on the nation for its failure to remove slavery from the land; and it was every American's duty not only to accept the elimination of slavery but to reunite the nation and forgive his or her fellow man.

Lincoln was shot by John Wilkes Booth on April 14, 1865, and died the following day.

Chapter 1

LEADERSHIP

—⋙—

Before he was elected president in 1860, Lincoln had received little formal education, no administrative training, and had held only one term in a national office, as a congressman from Illinois. His only military experience had been a few weeks of service in the state militia during the Black Hawk War.

Many of the North's most powerful political leaders wanted to let the South secede. Lincoln, however, was absolutely committed to maintenance of the Union—and made every task subservient to this cause. Although it is significant that he successfully led the war effort, to include hiring and firing generals and cabinet members until he found those who succeeded, his most important accomplishment probably was the continuous motivation of the people for the cause, in spite of the terrible losses of the long war.

$\mathcal{I}$t was in the oath I took that I would, to the best of my ability, preserve, protect, and defend the Constitution of the United States. I could not take the office without taking the oath. Nor was it my view that I might take an oath to get power, and break the oath in using the power.[1]

★ ★ ★

$\mathcal{I}$ don't know but that God has created some one man great enough to comprehend the whole of this stupendous crisis and transaction from beginning to end, and endowed him with sufficient wisdom to manage and direct it. I confess I do not fully understand, and foresee it all. But I am placed here where I am obliged to the best of my poor ability to deal with it.[2]

★ ★ ★

$\mathcal{I}$ am decided; my course is fixed; my path is blazed. The Union and the Constitution shall be preserved and the laws enforced at every and at all hazards. I expect the people to sustain me. They have never yet forsaken any true man.[3]

$\mathcal{I}$n your hands, my dissatisfied fellow-countrymen, and not in mine, is the momentous issue of civil war. The government will not assail you. You can have no conflict without being yourselves the aggressors. You have no oath registered in heaven to destroy the government, while I shall have the most solemn one to "preserve, protect, and defend it."[4]

★ ★ ★

$\mathcal{N}$either let us be slandered from our duty by false accusations against us, nor frightened from it by menaces of destruction to the government, nor of dungeons to ourselves. Let us have faith that right makes might; and in that faith let us to the end dare to do our duty as we understand it.[5]

15

He would listen to everybody; he would hear everybody; but he rarely, if ever, asked for opinions. As a politician and as president, he arrived at all his conclusions from his own reflections, and when his opinion was once formed, he never doubted that it was right.[6]

Leonard Swett, close friend of Lincoln

Think nothing of me—take no thought for the political fate of any man whomsoever, but come back to the truths that are in the Declaration of Independence. ... I charge you to drop every paltry and insignificant thought for any man's success. It is nothing; I am nothing; Judge Douglas is nothing. But do not destroy that immortal emblem of Humanity—the Declaration of American Independence.[7]

The Union must be preserved, and hence, all indispen- sable means must be employed.[8]

$\mathcal{I}$ attempt no compliment to my own sagacity. I claim not to have controlled events, but confess plainly that events have controlled me. Now, at the end of three years' struggle, the nation's condition is not what either party, or any man, devised or expected. God alone can claim it.[9]

★ ★ ★

$\mathcal{L}$et there be no compromise on the question of extending slavery. If there be, all our labor is lost, and ere long, must be done again. The dangerous ground—that into which some of our friends have a hankering to run—is Popular Sovereignty. Have none of it. Stand firm.[10]

$\mathcal{B}$y general law, life and limb must be protected, yet often a limb must be amputated to save a life; but a life is never wisely given to save a limb. I felt that measures otherwise unconstitutional might become lawful by becoming indispensable to the preservation of the Constitution through the preservation of the nation. Right or wrong, I assumed this ground and now avow it.[11]

—∾∾—

In small and unimportant matters, Mr. Lincoln was so yielding that many thought his excessive amiability was born of weakness. But, in matters of vital importance, he was firm as a rock. Neither Congress nor his cabinet could, in the slightest degree, influence his action on great questions, against the convictions of his patriotic judgment.[12]

John B. Alley, congressman and friend of Lincoln

With all his awkwardness of manner, and utter disregard of social conventionalities that seemed to invite familiarity, there was something about Abraham Lincoln that enforced respect. No man presumed on the apparent invitation to be other than respectful.[13]

Donn Piatt, soldier and journalist

—∽∽—

*I*f I were to try to read, much less answer, all the attacks made on me, this shop might as well be closed for any other business. I do the very best I know how—the very best I can; and I mean to keep doing so until the end. If the end brings me out all right, what is said against me won't amount to anything. If the end brings me out wrong, ten thousand angels swearing I was right would make no difference.[15]

**Even in [Lincoln's] freest moments one always felt
the presence of a will and an intellectual power
which maintained the ascendancy of the president.
He never posed or put on airs or attempted to make
any particular impression; but he was always con-
scious of his own ideas and purposes, even in his
most unreserved moments.**[16]

Charles A. Dana, assistant secretary of war in Lincoln administration

★ ★ ★

Towering genius disdains a beaten path.[14]

Chapter 2

HONESTY

Lincoln earned the nickname "Honest Abe" when he was a young man working as a store clerk. It is recorded that if he realized he had accidentally shortchanged a customer a few pennies, he thought nothing of closing up the shop and walking several miles to deliver the correct change. Recognizing Lincoln's honesty, people were soon asking him to act as judge or referee in various things. He became a popular arbiter of wrestling matches, horse races, and petty squabbles.

Whether as a clerk in a country store, representative in the state legislature, or lawyer in court, Lincoln dealt honestly with everyone. Throughout his entire career in politics and public service, he was extremely proud of his reputation and took great care to justify the "Honest Abe" sobriquet.

On the underlying principles of truth and justice his will was as firm as steel and as tenacious as iron.[1]

William Herndon, law partner and close friend of Lincoln

I planted myself upon the truth and the truth only, so far as I knew it, or could be brought to know it.[2]

★ ★ ★

I have always wanted to deal with everyone I meet candidly and honestly. If I have made any assertion not warranted by facts, and it is pointed out to me, I will withdraw it cheerfully.[3]

★ ★ ★

I made a point of honor and conscience in all things to stick to my word, especially if others had been induced to act on it.[4]

$\mathcal{R}$esolve to be honest at all events; and if in your judgment you cannot be an honest lawyer, resolve to be honest without being a lawyer. Choose some other occupation, rather than one in the choosing of which you do, in advance, consent to be a knave.[5]

—∽∽—

I shall have my hands full. He is the strong man of his party—full of wit, facts, dates—and the best stump speaker, with his droll ways and dry jokes, in the West. He is as honest as he is shrewd, and if I beat him my victory will be hardly won.[6]

Sen. Stephen A. Douglas, upon hearing that Lincoln would be his political adversary in Illinois's 1858 U.S. Senate race

25

$\mathcal{I}$ wish at all times in no way to practice any fraud upon the House or the committee, and I also desire to do nothing which may be very disagreeable to any of the members [of Congress].[7]

★ ★ ★

$\mathcal{I}$ don't want to be unjustly accused of dealing illiberally or unfairly with an adversary, either in court, or in a political canvass, or anywhere else. I would despise myself if I supposed myself ready to deal less liberally with an adversary than I was willing to be treated myself.[8]

★ ★ ★

$\mathcal{I}$ am glad of all the support I can get anywhere, if I can get it without practicing any deception to obtain it.[9]

I do not state a thing and say I know it when I do not ... I mean to put a case no stronger than the truth will allow.[10]

Mr. Lincoln … is almost monomaniac on the subject of honesty.[11]

Mary Todd Lincoln, when writing a friend
about her husband's insistence on telling the truth

*I*f it is decreed that I should go down because of this speech, then let me go down linked to the truth—let me die in the advocacy of what is just and right.[12]

★ ★ ★

*S*tand with anybody that stands right. Stand with him while he is right, and part with him when he goes wrong.[13]

28

His moral character stands among us here without reproach or blemish. I have known him for twenty years, and latterly as circumstances have made him more prominent I have become well acquainted with him, and have watched the course of public opinion in these parts, both among his friends and his foes. … Abraham Lincoln has been here all the time, consulting and consulted by all classes, all parties, and on all subjects of political interest, with men of every degree of corruption and yet I have never heard even an enemy accuse him of intentional dishonesty or corruption. … He has stood before the community here the man of uncorrupted if not incorruptible integrity, and to be able to say that of any man who has mingled as freely with Illinois politics and politicians as Mr. Lincoln has is glory enough for one man.[14]

Rev. Albert Hale, pastor of the Second Presbyterian Church of Springfield

$\mathcal{I}$ have never tried to conceal my opinions, nor tried to deceive anyone in reference to them. [15]

★ ★ ★

$\mathcal{Y}$ou must remember that some things legally right are not morally right. [16]

—∿∿—

Mr. Lincoln's judgment was final in all that region of the country. People relied implicitly upon his honesty, integrity, and impartiality. [17]

Robert B. Rutledge, resident of
New Salem when Lincoln lived there

$\mathcal{T}$ruth is generally the best vindication against slander.[18]

★ ★ ★

$\mathcal{I}$n very truth he [a deceased associate of Lincoln] was the noblest work of God—an honest man.[19]

—ᴍ—

The framework for [Lincoln's] mental and moral being was honesty, and a wrong cause was poorly defended by him.[20]

Judge David Douglas, in whose court
Lincoln practiced law for fourteen years

You have nominated a very able and very honest man.[21]

Stephen A. Douglas, upon hearing that Lincoln had been nominated by the 1860 Republican Convention for president of the United States

Chapter 3

FAITH

Lincoln's faith is frequently debated by historians. Some say Lincoln was an unbeliever, or at least a skeptic, of Christianity. Many say he was a "deeply religious" man who sought God's guidance daily.

Lincoln never formally joined a church, but he knew the Bible very well. He memorized a great deal of Scripture and could quote it better than many ministers of the Gospel. Even though Lincoln went through a period of skepticism as a young man, his confidence in the Gospel grew significantly as he matured and survived life's hardships. By the time he had become president, Lincoln was a man of deep faith.

As president, Lincoln frequently discussed his dependence on God, acknowledging that his most earnest prayer was to determine the Lord's will so that he could follow it.

𝒲hatever shall appear to be God's will I will do. [1]

★ ★ ★

𝒯he will of God prevails. In great contests each party claims to act in accordance with the will of God. Both may be, and one must be, wrong. God cannot be for and against the same thing at the same time. In the present civil war it is quite possible that God's purpose is something different from the purpose of either party; and yet the human instrumentalities, working just as they do, are of the best adaptation to effect his purpose. I am almost ready to say that this is probably true; that God wills this contest, and wills that it shall not end yet. [2]

★ ★ ★

𝒥f we do right God will be with us, and if God is with us we cannot fail. [3]

$\mathcal{A}$mid the greatest difficulties of my Administration, when I could not see any other resort, I would place my whole reliance in God, knowing that all would go well, and that He would decide for the right. [4]

★ ★ ★

$\mathcal{I}$ am not at all concerned about that [that the Lord was on the North's side in the war], for I know the Lord is always on the side of the *right*. But it is my constant anxiety and prayer that I and this nation should be on the Lord's side. [5]

★ ★ ★

$\mathcal{T}$here is no contending against the Will of God; but still there is some difficulty in ascertaining, and applying it, to particular cases. [6]

As [Lincoln] became involved in matters of the greatest importance, full of great responsibility and great doubt, a feeling of religious reverence, a belief in God and his justice and overruling power increased with him. … He believed in the great laws of truth, and the rigid discharge of duty, his accountability to God, the ultimate triumph of the right and the overthrow of wrong. If his religion were to be judged by the lines and rules of Church creeds, he would fall far short of the standard; but if by the higher rule of purity of conduct, of honesty of motive, of unyielding fidelity to the right, and acknowledging God as the supreme ruler, then he filled all the requirements of true devotion, and his whole life was a life of love to God, and love of his neighbor as of himself.[7]

Leonard Swett, close friend of Lincoln

$\mathcal{W}$e are indeed going through a trial—a fiery trial. In the very responsible position in which I happen to be placed, being a humble instrument in the hands of our Heavenly Father, as I am, and as we all are, to work out His great purposes, I have desired that all my works and acts may be according to His will, and that it might be so, I have sought His aid—but if after endeavoring to do my best in the light which He affords me, I find my efforts fail, I must believe that for some purpose unknown to me, He wills it otherwise.[8]

★ ★ ★

$\mathcal{O}$ur political problem now is "Can we, as a nation, continue together permanently—forever—half slave, and half free?" The problem is too mighty for me. May God, in his mercy, superintend the solution.[9]

The purposes of the Almighty are perfect, and must prevail, though we erring mortals may fail to accurately perceive them in advance. We hoped for a happy termination of this terrible war long before this; but God knows best, and has ruled otherwise. We shall yet acknowledge His wisdom, and our own error therein. Meanwhile we must work earnestly in the best lights He gives us, trusting that so working still conduces to the great ends He ordains. Surely He intends some great good to follow this mighty convulsion, which no mortal could make, and no mortal could stay.[10]

★   ★   ★

I should be the most presumptuous blockhead upon this foot-stool if I for one day thought that I should discharge the duties which have come upon me, since I came to this place, without the aid and enlightenment of One who is stronger and wiser than all others.[11]

38

It is most cheering and encouraging for me to know that in the efforts which I have made and am making for the restoration of a righteous peace to our country, I am upheld and sustained by the good wishes and prayers of God's people. No one is more deeply than myself aware that without His favor our highest wisdom is but as foolishness and that our most strenuous efforts would avail nothing in the shadow of His displeasure. [12]

He never joined a Church; but still, as I believe, he was a religious man by nature. [13]

Mary Todd Lincoln

$\mathcal{I}$t is the duty of nations as well as of men to own their dependence upon the overruling power of God; to confess their sins and transgressions, in humble sorrow, yet with assured hope that genuine repentance will lead to mercy and pardon; and to recognize the sublime truth, announced in the Holy Scriptures and proven by all history, that those nations only are blessed whose God is the Lord. ...

We have been preserved, these many years, in peace and prosperity. We have grown in numbers, wealth, and power as no other nation has ever grown; but we have forgotten God. We have forgotten the gracious hand which has preserved us in peace, and multiplied and enriched and strengthened us; and we have vainly imagined, in the deceitfulness of our hearts, that all these blessings were produced by some superior wisdom and virtue of our own. Intoxicated with unbroken success, we have become too self-sufficient to feel the necessity of redeeming and preserving grace, too proud to pray to the God that made us. ...

It behooves us, then, to humble ourselves before the offended Power, to confess our national sins, and to pray for clemency and forgiveness. [14]

—From Lincoln's Proclamation Appointing a National Fast Day, March 30, 1863

40

Take all of this Book [the Bible] upon reason that you can and the balance on faith, and you will live and die a happier and better man.[15]

*I*n regards to this great Book [the Bible], I have but to say, it is the best gift God has given to men. All the good Savior gave to this world was communicated through this Book. But for it we could not know right from wrong. All things most desirable for man's welfare, here and hereafter, are to be found portrayed in it. [16]

★ ★ ★

*M*y Friends: … Without the assistance of that Divine Being who ever attended him, I cannot succeed. With that assistance, I cannot fail. Trusting in Him who can go with me, and remain with you, and be everywhere for good, let us confidently hope that all will yet be well. To His care commending you, as I hope in your prayers you will commend me, I bid you an affectionate farewell. [17]

　　—from Lincoln's farewell speech to the citizens of
　　Springfield, Illinois, on February 11, 1861

Chapter 4

THE PEOPLE

Lincoln had tremendous faith in the people. Having grown up in the Midwestern wilderness, he had watched his family and neighbors overcome hardships typical of pioneers in the early nineteenth century. He believed that the American people were the most intelligent, industrious, and resourceful people in the world. Convinced that their character was reflected in the democratic government they had formed, he believed that as long as the people retained "their virtue and vigilance," they could never be successfully misled by any corrupt politician or sophist.

Lincoln believed in the people because he knew the people. One of his greatest qualities as a leader was his ability to recognize the strengths and weaknesses of others, and use each individual effectively for the benefit of the nation.

$\mathcal{I}$ think of the whole people of this nation; they will ever do well if well done by.[1]

★ ★ ★

$\mathcal{T}$he people will save their government if the government itself will do its part only indifferently well.[2]

★ ★ ★

$\mathcal{W}$hy should there not be a patient confidence in the ultimate justice of the people? Is there any better or equal hope in the world?[3]

★ ★ ★

$\mathcal{I}$ appeal to you [the people] again to constantly bear in mind that not with politicians, not with Presidents, not with office-seekers, but with you is the question, "Shall the Union, shall the liberties of this country, be preserved to the latest generations?"[4]

At what point then is the approach of danger to be expected? I answer, if it ever reach us it must spring up amongst us; it cannot come from abroad. If destruction be our lot we must ourselves be its author and finisher. As a nation of freemen we must live through all time or die by suicide.[5]

★ ★ ★

This is essentially a people's contest. On the side of the Union it is a struggle for maintaining in the world that form and substance of government whose leading object is to elevate the condition of men—to lift artificial weights from all shoulders; to clear the paths of laudable pursuit for all; to afford all an unfettered start, and a fair chance in the race of life. … I am most happy to believe that the plain people understand and appreciate this …[6]

He [Lincoln] prized the suggestions of the unso-phisticated people more than what was called state-craft or political wisdom. He really believed that the voice of the people in our emergency was [the] next thing to the voice of God.[7]

Joseph Gillespie, old friend and legal associate of Lincoln

★ ★ ★

It is, fellow-citizens, for the whole American people, and not for one single man alone, to advance the great cause of the Union and the Constitution. And in a country like this, where every man bears on his face the marks of intelligence, where every man's clothing, if I may so speak, shows signs of comfort, and every dwelling signs of happiness and contentment, where schools and churches abound on every side, the Union can never be in danger.[8]

*I*n leaving
the people's
business in
their hands,
we cannot
be wrong.[9]

The integrity of our country and the stability of our government mainly depend … on the loyalty, virtue, patriotism, and intelligence of the American people.[10]

★ ★ ★

While the people retain their virtue and vigilance, no administration by any extreme of wickedness or folly can very seriously injure the government in the short space of four years.[11]

★ ★ ★

This … indicates an earnest desire on the part of the whole people, without regard to political differences, to save—not the country, because the country will save itself—but to save the institutions under which, in the last three-quarters of a century, we have grown to a great, an intelligent, and a happy people—the greatest, the most intelligent, and the happiest people in the world.[12]

But take men as a whole—I think he [Lincoln] thought better of them than they deserve. He had more faith in mankind, the masses, than any other man I ever knew. [13]

Isaac Arnold, old friend and early biographer of Lincoln

ℐt is true … that very great responsibility rests upon me in the position to which the votes of the American people have called me. I am deeply sensible of that weighty responsibility. … I turn, then, and look to the American people, and to that God who has never forsaken them. [14]

𝒥f the people remain right, your public men can never betray you. … Cultivate and protect that sentiment [that the principles of liberty are eternal] and your ambitious leaders will be reduced to the position of servants instead of masters. [15]

★ ★ ★

𝒜llow me to say that you, as a portion of the great American people, need only to maintain your composure, stand up to your sober convictions of right, to your obligations to the Constitution, and act in accordance with those sober convictions, and the clouds now on the horizon will be dispelled, and we shall have a bright and glorious future … [16]

We are bound together in Christianity, civilization, and patriotism, and our attachment to our country and our whole country. While some of us may differ in political opinions, still we are all united in one feeling for the Union. We all believe in the maintenance of the Union, of every star and stripe of the glorious flag.[17]

★ ★ ★

Encompassed by vast difficulties as I am, nothing shall be wanting on my part, if sustained by God and the American people.[18]

★ ★ ★

The people know their rights, and they are never slow to assert and maintain them, when they are invaded.[19]

The trust which Abraham Lincoln had in himself and in the people was surprising and grand, but it was also enlightened and well founded. He knew the American people better than they knew themselves, and his trust was based upon this knowledge.[20]

Frederick Douglass, former slave and
famous abolitionist Lincoln befriended

The people of these United States are the rightful masters of both congresses and courts, not to overthrow the Constitution, but to overthrow the men who pervert the Constitution.[21]

★ ★ ★

It is not the qualified voters, but the qualified voters who choose to vote, that constitute the political power of the State.[22]

52

Lincoln was the apostle of the common people. Their rights, their conditions, their hardships, their opportunities, their aspirations, their hopes, their joys and their sorrows—all these were subjects upon which his mind brooded and sought to work out plans for their betterment and happiness. No man ever knew the common people better than he, or was closer in sympathy with them. Having sprung from the innumerable common throng, his heart never ceased to beat in sympathy with them. Besides, he was endowed with that best sense— common sense. This, with his broad, clear grasp of every subject that touched the interest of the masses, made him preeminently the advocate of the rights of the common people.[23]

Judge Owen T. Reeves, soldier and legal scholar of Lincoln's day

Chapter 5

KINDNESS

There are many stories about Lincoln's kindness. As a young-ster and even as a young man, he was always rescuing friends or animals from calamity. As a lawyer, he many times offered to argue the case of some unfortunate person who could not afford counsel. Sometimes, when he thought he had been overpaid for legal work, he would return the money that he perceived to be in excess of what he was due.

But perhaps the supreme example of Lincoln's kindness was his willingness as president to work late hours, poring over the army's court-martial cases in which soldiers had been sentenced to be shot. He read each one diligently, look-ing for an excuse to pardon the man and spare his life. He continued to do this despite the protests of his generals, who claimed he was undermining discipline.

$\mathcal{I}$ am a patient man—always willing to forgive on the Christian terms of repentance; and also to give ample time for repentance.[1]

★ ★ ★

$\mathcal{I}$ shall do nothing in malice. What I deal with is too vast for malicious dealing.[2]

★ ★ ★

$\mathcal{I}$ can only say that I have acted upon my best convictions, without selfishness or malice, and that by the help of God I shall continue to do so.[3]

★ ★ ★

$\mathcal{S}$ome of my generals complain that I impair discipline by my frequent pardons and reprieves; but it rests me, after a day's hard work, that I can find some excuse for saving some poor fellow's life, and I shall go to bed happy tonight as I think how joyous the signing of this name will make himself, his family, and friends.[4]

I must say, and I am proud to say, that I never was treated by anyone with more kindness and cordiality than was shown me by the great and good man, Abraham Lincoln, by the grace of God president of the United States ...[5]

Sojourner Truth, former slave who visited
Lincoln at the White House in October 1864

★ ★ ★

Human nature will not change. In any future great national trial, compared with the men of this, we shall have as weak and as strong, as silly and as wise, as bad and as good. Let us therefore study the incidents of this, as philosophy to learn wisdom from, and none of them as wrongs to be revenged.[6]

★ ★ ★

I have an irrepressible desire to live till I can be assured that the world is a little better for my having lived in it.[7]

$\mathcal{I}$ am loath to close. We are not enemies but friends. We must not be enemies. Though passion may have strained, it must not break our bonds of affection. The mystic chords of memory, stretching from every battlefield and patriot grave to every living heart and hearthstone all over this broad land, will yet swell the chorus of the Union when again touched, as surely they will be, by the better angels of our nature.[8]

★ ★ ★

$\mathcal{O}$n principle I dislike an oath which requires a man to swear he has not done wrong. It rejects the Christian principle of forgiveness on terms of repentance. I think it is enough if the man does no wrong hereafter.[9]

—◊◊◊—

He was one of the few great rulers whose wisdom increased with his power, and whose spirit grew gentler and tenderer as his triumphs were multiplied. [10]

James A. Garfield, twentieth U.S. president;
a soldier and then a politician in Lincoln's day

58

On the whole, my impression is that mercy bears richer fruits than any other attribute.[11]

He would be just as kind and generous as his judgment would let him be—no more. If he ever deviated from this rule, it was to save life.[12]

Leonard Swett

*I*n all our rejoicings, let us neither express nor cherish any hard feelings toward any citizen who, by his vote, has differed with us. Let us at all times remember that all American citizens are brothers of common country, and should do well together in the bonds of fraternal feeling.[13]

★ ★ ★

*I*t is no pleasure to me to triumph over anyone.[14]

$\mathcal{I}$f a man had more than one life, I think a little hanging would not hurt this one, but after he is once dead we cannot bring him back, no matter how sorry we may be, so the boy shall be pardoned. [15]

—ɯ—

No man clothed with such vast power ever wielded it more tenderly and more forbearingly. No man holding in his hands the key of life and death ever pardoned so many offenders, and so easily. [16]

Schuyler Colfax, vice president in the first Grant administration

Chapter 6

LIBERTY

—◦◦◦—

Lincoln recognized that liberty meant different things to different Americans, and he fought hard to preserve the liberties he believed the founding fathers had intended. He did not agree with Stephen A. Douglas, who contended that the writers of the Declaration of Independence never intended for African-Americans to be included when they said "all men" were "created equal." Lincoln believed that everyone, regardless of their race, at least had the right to "eat the bread they earned."

Lincoln also believed that although the framers of the government originally allowed slavery, it was the intention of the founding fathers to one day provide life, liberty, and the pursuit of happiness equally to all—regardless of their race. The love of liberty, and his fear that the American people may one day lose it, motivated Lincoln more than anything else.

The fight must go on. The cause of civil liberty must not be surrendered at the end of one or even one hundred defeats.[1]

★ ★ ★

I believe the declaration that "all men are created equal" is the great fundamental principle upon which our free institutions rest.[2]

★ ★ ★

Those who deny freedom to others deserve it not for themselves; and, under a just God, cannot long retain it.[3]

★ ★ ★

Our reliance is in the love of liberty which God has planted in our bosoms. Our defense is in the preservation of the spirit which prized liberty as the heritage of all men, in all lands, everywhere. Destroy this spirit and you have planted the seeds of despotism around your own doors. Familiarize yourselves with the chains of bondage, and you are preparing your own limbs to wear them.[4]

$\mathcal{T}$he world has never had a good definition of the word *liberty*, and the American people, just now, are much in want of one. We all declare for liberty; but in using the same word we do not all mean the same thing. With some the word *liberty* may mean for each man to do as he pleases with himself, and the product of his labor; while with others the same word may mean for some men to do as they please with other men, and the product of other men's labor. Here are two, not only different, but incompatible things, called by the same name, liberty.[5]

★ ★ ★

$\mathcal{W}$hat is it that we hold most dear amongst us? Our own liberty and prosperity. What has ever threatened our liberty and prosperity, save and except this institution of slavery?[6]

In all my interviews with Mr. Lincoln I was impressed with his entire freedom from popular prejudice against the colored race. He was the first great man that I talked with in the United States freely, who in no single instance reminded me of the difference between himself and myself, of the difference of color. … Then, too, there was another feeling that I had with reference to him, and that was that while I felt in his presence I was in the presence of a very great man, as great as the greatest, I felt as though I could go and put my hand on him if I wanted to, to put my hand on his shoulder. Of course I did not do it, but I felt that I could. I felt as though I was in the presence of a big brother, and that there was safety in his atmosphere.[7]

Frederick Douglass

There is something back of these, entwining itself more closely about the human heart. That something is the principle of "Liberty to all"—the principle that clears the path for all, gives hope to all, and, by consequence, enterprise and industry to all.[8]

They were the pillars of the temple of liberty; and now, that they have crumbled away, that temple must fall, unless we, their descendants, supply their places with other pillars, hewn from the solid quarry of sober reason.[9]

★　★　★

My friends, I have detained you about as long as I desired to do, and I have only to say, let us discard all this quibbling about this man and the other man—this race and that race and the other race being inferior, and therefore they must be placed in an inferior position. Let us discard all these things, and unite as one people throughout this land, until we shall once more stand up declaring that all men are created equal.[10]

★　★　★

I want every man to have a chance, and I believe a black man is entitled to it—in which he can better his condition …[11]

Theirs [our American ancestors] was the task—and nobly they performed it—to possess themselves, and through themselves us, of this goodly land, and to uprear upon its hills and its valleys a political edifice of liberty and equal rights; 'tis ours only to transmit these—the former unprofaned by the foot of an invader, the latter undecayed by the lapse of time and untorn by usurpation—to the latest generation that fate shall permit the world to know.[12]

★ ★ ★

Our progress in degeneracy appears to me to be pretty rapid. As a nation we began by declaring that "all men are created equal." We now practically read it "all men are created equal, except Negroes." When the Know-Nothings get control, it will read "all men are created equal, except Negroes and foreigners and Catholics." When it comes to this, I shall prefer emigrating to some country where they make no pretense of loving liberty—to Russia, for instance, where despotism can be taken pure and without the base alloy of hypocrisy.[13]

(The Know-Nothing Party was a "nativist" political party in the 1850s)

His great mission was to accomplish two things: first, to save his country from dismemberment and ruin; and second, to free his country from the great crime of slavery. To do one or the other, or both, he must have the earnest sympathy and the powerful cooperation of his loyal fellow-countrymen. Without this primary and essential condition to success his efforts must have been vain and utterly fruitless. Had he put the abolition of slavery before the salvation of the Union, he would have inevitably driven from him a powerful class of the American people and rendered resistance to rebellion impossible. Viewed from the genuine abolition ground, Mr. Lincoln seemed tardy, cold, dull, and indifferent; but measuring him by the sentiment of his country, a sentiment he was bound as a statesman to consult, he was swift, zealous, radical, and determined.[14]

Frederick Douglass

Although volume upon volume is written to prove slavery a good thing, we never hear of the man who wishes to take the good of it, by being a slave himself.[15]

★ ★ ★

That is the issue that will continue in this country when these poor tongues of Judge Douglas and myself shall be silent. It is the eternal struggle between these two principles—right and wrong—throughout the world. They are the two principles that have stood face to face from the beginning of time; and will ever continue to struggle. The one is the common right of humanity, and the other the divine right of kings. It is the same principle in whatever shape it develops itself. It is the same spirit that says, "You toil and work and earn bread, and I'll eat it."[16]

★ ★ ★

Let every American, every lover of liberty, every well-wisher to his posterity, swear by the blood of the Revolution never to violate in the least particular the laws of the country, and never to tolerate their violation by others.[17]

He was advised long before 1860, by some of his more intimate friends, that his positions on the subject of slavery and human rights would be prejudicial to his party and to himself personally. He paid no attention to such admonitions. The question with him was whether the thing was right, and not what his friends may have thought about the expediency of it.[18]

Judge Lawrence Weldon, legal associate of Lincoln

But the inevitable topic to which he returned with the most frequency, and to which he clung with all the grasp of his soul, was the practical character of the Declaration of Independence in announcing the Liberty and Equality of all men.[19]

Charles Sumner, senator and friend of Lincoln

Chapter 7

COMMON SENSE

Those people who knew Lincoln were always impressed with his abundant common sense. Lincoln himself claimed that although his mind worked very slowly, it was like steel—once something had been etched into it, it could not be removed. Lincoln was fond of repeating many of the anecdotes and jewels of wisdom he had accumulated over the years in speeches and letters he authored.

Some of the witticisms that are attributed to Lincoln today were probably common expressions of his day, but it is difficult to separate these from those that originated with him. Regardless of whether they were started by Lincoln or someone else, he used each of these gems to communicate a worthy point to the listener, and today they represent timeless wisdom worth remembering.

When I have friends who disagree with each other, I am very slow to take sides in their quarrel.[1]

★ ★ ★

When one is embarrassed, usually the shortest way to get through with it is to quit talking or thinking about it, and go at something else.[2]

★ ★ ★

Men are not flattered by being shown that there has been a difference of purpose between the Almighty and them.[3]

★ ★ ★

Common-looking people are the best in the world; that is the reason the Lord makes so many of them.[4]

Quarrel not at all. No man resolved to make the most of himself can spare time for personal contention. Still less can he afford to take all the consequences, including the vitiating of his temper and the loss of self-control. Yield larger things to which you can show no more than equal right; and yield lesser ones, though clearly your own. Better give your path to a dog than be bitten by him in contesting for the right. Even killing the dog would not cure the bite.[5]

★ ★ ★

I am never easy now, when I am handling a thought, till I have bounded it north and bounded it south, and bounded it east and bounded it west.[6]

★ ★ ★

Half-finished work generally proves to be labor lost.[7]

The better part of one's life consists of his friendships.[8]

★ ★ ★

The loss of enemies does not compensate for the loss of friends.[9]

—∿—

The characteristic that struck me most about [Lincoln] was his superabundance of common sense. His power of managing men, of deciding and avoiding difficult questions, surpassed that of any man I ever met. A keen insight of human nature had been cultivated by the trials and struggles of his early life. He knew the people and how to reach them better than any man of his time.[10]

Chauncey M. Depew, state representative
from New York and orator during Lincoln's time

A man has no time to spend half his life in quarrels.[11]

$\mathcal{P}$ersuade your neighbor to compromise whenever you can. [12]

★ ★ ★

$\mathcal{I}$f you would win a man to your cause, first convince him that you are his sincere friend. Therein is a drop of honey that catches his heart, which … when once gained, you will find but little trouble in convincing his judgment of the justice of your cause. [13]

★ ★ ★

$\mathcal{B}$ad promises are better broken than kept. [14]

—◯—

Lincoln was master of statement. Few have equaled him in the ability to strip a truth of surplus verbiage and present it in its naked strength. [15]

William Jennings Bryan, politician
and orator of the late nineteenth century

All creation is a mine, and every man, a miner.[16]

★ ★ ★

Common people ... are more easily influenced and informed through the medium of a broad illustration than in any other way.[17]

★ ★ ★

If you make a bad bargain, hug it all the tighter.[18]

★ ★ ★

Nothing valuable can be lost by taking time. If there be an object to hurry any of you, in hot haste, to a step which you would never take deliberately, that object will be frustrated by taking time; but no good object can be frustrated by it.[19]

Even those who only knew him through his public utterances obtained a tolerably clear idea of his character and his personality. The image of the man went through his words, and those who read them, knew him. [20]

Frederick Douglass

What is to be will be, and no cares of ours can arrest nor reverse the decree. [21]

★ ★ ★

As a general rule, I abstain from reading the reports of attacks upon myself, wishing not to be provoked by that to which I cannot properly offer an answer. [22]

Chapter 8

CHARACTER

The dictionary tells us that character is the moral or ethical structure of a person. With the possible exception of George Washington, Lincoln is admired for his character more than any other American leader. Honesty, honor, wisdom, vision, kindness—all of these qualities are attributed to Lincoln.

Even so, Lincoln was not universally admired in his lifetime. In fact, he was hated by many. However, by the time he had begun his second term as president, he had developed the respect of friends and enemies alike. Both friend and foe recognized that he had fought his way up from poverty and ignorance. Many saw him as a patient, benevolent leader who brought the nation through its most difficult hour. Most realized that he endured a great deal of hostility on the part of his fellow man and rarely returned anything but kindness.

𝘈 man's character is like a tree and his reputation like its shadow; the shadow is what we think of it; the tree is the real thing.[1]

★ ★ ★

𝘐 [wish to be] so clear that no honest man can misunderstand me and no dishonest one successfully misrepresent me.[2]

★ ★ ★

𝘐 have not permitted myself, gentlemen, to conclude that I am the best man in the country; but I am reminded, in this connection, of a story of an old Dutch farmer, who remarked to a companion once that "It was not best to swap horses when crossing streams."[3]

★ ★ ★

𝘐 have endured a great deal of ridicule without much malice; and have received a great deal of kindness, not quite free from ridicule. I am used to it.[4]

The world shall know that I will keep my faith to friends and enemies, come what will.[5]

★ ★ ★

I want in all cases to do right, and most particularly so in all cases with women.[6]

—〰—

The beauty of his character was its entire simplicity. … True to nature, true to himself, he was true to everybody and everything about and around him. When he was ignorant on any subject, no matter how simple it might make him appear he was always willing to acknowledge it. His whole aim in life was to be true to himself and being true to himself he could be false to no one.[7]

Joshua Speed, one of Lincoln's closest friends

𝔐any free countries have lost their liberty; and ours may lose hers; but if she shall, be it my proudest plume, not that I was the last to desert, but that I never deserted her.[8]

★ ★ ★

𝔐ost certainly I intend no injustice to any, and if I have done any I deeply regret it.[9]

—ᴍ—

To me he always seemed to be a very great man. In all the qualities of true greatness of character and mind he was the equal, if not the superior, of all the great statesmen I have ever known. Of all these public men, none seemed to have so little pride of opinion. He was always learning and did not adhere to views which he found to be erroneous, simply because he had once formed and held them.[10]

John B. Alley, U.S. Congressman from Massachusetts

At every
step we
must be
true to
the main
purpose.[11]

$\mathcal{I}$ have never done an official act with a view to promote my personal aggrandizement, and I don't like to begin now.[12]

—m—

As a political leader he was actuated in his movements by strong convictions of duty, and had great power in convincing people of the righteousness of his cause. No man could stand in his presence and hear him without feeling sure of the honesty of his purposes and declarations, or of the strength of his arguments in behalf of whatever cause he championed.[13]

Shelby Cullom, senator and friend of Lincoln

★ ★ ★

$\mathcal{I}$ am very sure that if I do not go away from here a wiser man, I shall go away a better man, for having learned here what a very poor sort of a man I am.[14]

$\mathcal{I}$ am very little inclined on any occasion to say anything unless I hope to produce some good by it. [15]

★ ★ ★

$\mathcal{I}$ do not consider that I have ever accomplished anything without God; and if it is His will that I must die by the hand of an assassin, I must be resigned. I must do my duty as I see it, and leave the rest with God. [16]

★ ★ ★

$\mathcal{W}$hatever woman may cast her lot with mine, should any ever do so, it is my intention to do all in my power to make her happy and contented; and there is nothing I can imagine that would make me more unhappy than to fail in the effort. [17]

★ ★ ★

$\mathcal{I}$mportant principles may and must be inflexible. [18]

Lincoln ... has taught us, that no party or partisan can escape responsibility to the people; that no party advantage, or presumed party advantage, should ever swerve us from the plain path of duty, which is ever the path of honor and distinction. He emphasized his words by his daily life and deeds. He showed to the world by his lofty example, as well as by precept and maxim, that there are times when the voice of partisanship should be hushed and that of patriotism only be heeded.[19]

William McKinley, twenty-fifth president
of the United States; and a soldier in Lincoln's day

No men living are more worthy to be trusted than those who toil up from poverty—none less inclined to take, or touch, aught which they have not honestly earned.[20]

Chapter 9

DEMOCRACY

Lincoln's concept of democracy began with the Declaration of Independence—which he paraphrased as "No man is good enough to govern another man without that other's consent." He also believed that elected representatives are bound to carry out the known wishes of their constituents. He called this the "great living principle" of democracy.

Although he recognized that in allowing slavery, the Constitution had compromised the ideals expressed in the Declaration, he believed that this was an error that would be inevitably corrected. Consequently, he considered American democratic government, although imperfect, to be the best form of government known to man. He feared that if his generation did not preserve the Union, democracy would be forever lost and fail to benefit future generations.

Our government rests in public opinion. Whoever can change public opinion can change the government.[1]

★ ★ ★

I have never had a feeling, politically, that did not spring from the sentiments embodied in the Declaration of Independence.[2]

★ ★ ★

Most governments have been based, practically, on the denial of the equal rights of men. … Ours began by affirming those rights.[3]

★ ★ ★

I am exceedingly anxious that this Union, the Constitution, and the liberties of the people shall be perpetuated in accordance with the original idea for which that struggle was made, and I shall be most happy indeed if I shall be an humble instrument in the hands of the Almighty, and of this, His almost chosen people, for perpetuating the object of that great struggle.[4]

As I would not be a slave, so I would not be a master. This expresses my idea of democracy. Whatever differs from this, to the extent of the difference, is no democracy.[5]

★ ★ ★

The legitimate object of government is to do for a community of people whatever they need to have done, but cannot do at all, or cannot so well do, for themselves, in their separate and individual capacities. In all that the people can individually do as well for themselves, government ought not to interfere.[6]

—∞—

Lincoln believed in the uplifting of influences of free government, and that by giving all a chance we could get higher average results for the people than where governments are exclusive and opportunities are limited to the few. No American ever did so much as he to enlarge these opportunities.[7]

William McKinley

$\mathcal{I}$n this and like communities, public sentiment is everything. With public sentiment, nothing can fail; without it, nothing can succeed. Consequently he who molds public sentiment goes deeper than he who enacts statutes or pronounces decisions. He makes statutes and decisions possible or impossible to be executed. [8]

★ ★ ★

$\mathcal{I}$ trust I understand, and truly estimate, the right of self-government. My faith in the proposition that each man should do precisely as he pleases with all which is exclusively his own, lies at the foundation of the sense of justice there is in me. [9]

★ ★ ★

$\mathcal{I}$ go for all sharing the privileges of the government who assist in bearing its burdens. [10]

He did not hesitate, he did not doubt, he did not falter; but at once resolved that at whatever peril, at whatever cost, the union of the States would be preserved. A patriot himself, his faith was strong and unwavering in the patriotism of his countrymen. … but in the midst of all this tumult and timidity, and against all this, Abraham Lincoln was clear in his duty, and had an oath in heaven. He calmly and bravely heard the voice of doubt and fear all around him; but he had an oath in heaven, and there was not power enough on the earth to make this honest boatman, back-woodsman, and broad-handed splitter of rails evade or violate that sacred oath.[11]

Frederick Douglass

$\mathcal{I}$ consider the central idea pervading this struggle is the necessity that is upon us, of proving that popular government is not an absurdity. We must settle this question now, whether in a free government the minority have the right to break up the government whenever they choose. [12]

★   ★   ★

$\mathcal{A}$nd this issue embraces more than the fate of the United States. It presents to the whole family of man the question whether a constitutional republic or democracy—a government of the people by the same people—can or cannot maintain its territorial integrity against its own domestic foes. It presents the question whether discontented individuals, too few in numbers to control administration according to organic law in any case, can always, upon the pretenses made in this case, or on any other pretenses, or arbitrarily without any pretense, break up their government, and thus practically put an end to free government upon the earth. It forces us to ask: "Is there, in all republics, this inherent and fatal weakness?" "Must a government, of necessity, be too strong for the liberties of its own people, or too weak to maintain its own existence?" [13]

A free people, in times of peace and quiet—when pressed by no common dan-ger—naturally divide into parties. At such times, the man who is of nei-ther party, is not—cannot be—of any consequence.[14]

The true rule in determining to embrace or reject anything, is not whether it have any evil in it, but whether it have more of evil than of good. There are few things wholly evil or wholly good. Almost everything, especially of government policy, is an inseparable compound of the two; so that our best judgment of the preponderance between them is continually demanded.[15]

★ ★ ★

Finally, I insist, that if there is anything which it is the duty of the whole people to never entrust to any hands but their own, that thing is the preservation and perpetuity, of their own liberties, and institutions.[16]

★ ★ ★

Let every man remember that to violate the law is to trample on the blood of his father, and to tear the charter of his own and his children's liberty.[17]

$\mathcal{T}$o give the victory to the right, not bloody bullets, but peaceful ballots only, are necessary. Thanks to our good old constitution, and organization under it, these alone are necessary. It only needs that every right thinking man shall go to the polls and, without fear or prejudice, vote as he thinks. [18]

★   ★   ★

$\mathcal{I}$f the politicians and leaders of parties were as true as the people, there would be little fear that the peace of the country would be disturbed. I have been selected to fill an important office for a brief period, and am now, in your eyes, invested with an influence which will soon pass away; but should my administration prove to be a very wicked one, or what is more probable, a very foolish one, if you, the people, are but true to yourselves and to the Constitution, there is but little harm I can do, thank God! [19]

Chapter 10

PERSEVERANCE

—⊸⊸—

One of Lincoln's greatest strengths as a leader was his ability to identify the most important problem and concentrate every resource on solving it. He admitted that he was sometimes slow making up his mind as to what to do, but once he did, he never wavered regarding his purpose.

As president, Lincoln sought to "learn God's will" on important issues, and once he believed he'd determined that will, he never hesitated in following it. His commitment to maintenance of the Union is a prime example. He was willing to do anything, even ignore the Constitution, in order to maintain the sovereignty of the United States of America. He considered this equivalent to "sacrificing a limb" in order to "save a life."

Always bear in mind that your own resolution to succeed is more important than any other one thing.[1]

★ ★ ★

Must is the word. I know not how to aid you, save in the assurance of one of mature age, and much severe experience, that you can not fail, if you resolutely determine that you will not.[2]

★ ★ ★

By all means, don't say "if I can"; say "I will."[3]

★ ★ ★

I expect to maintain this contest until successful, or till I die, or am conquered, or my term expires, or Congress or the country forsakes me.[4]

    —*Lincoln talking about his effort to prosecute the war*

Whilst other boys were idling away their time, Lincoln was at home studdying [sic] hard.[5]

Nat Grigsby, boyhood friend of Lincoln and a soldier in the Civil War

—∞—

The probability that we may fall in the struggle ought not to deter us from the support of a cause we believe to be just.[6]

★ ★ ★

The way for a young man to rise, is to improve himself every way he can, never suspecting that anybody wishes to hinder him. Allow me to assure you, that suspicion and jealousy never did help any man in any situation. There may sometimes be ungenerous attempts to keep a young man down; and they will succeed, too, if he allows his mind to be diverted from its true channel to brood over the attempted injury.[7]

In his rise from the most abject poverty and igno-rance to a position of high usefulness and power, he taught the world one of the greatest of all lessons. In fighting his own battle up from obscurity and squalor, he fought the battle of every other individ-ual and race that is down, and so helped to pull up every other human who was down. People so often forget that by every inch that the lowest man crawls up he makes it easier for every other man to get up. Today, throughout the world, because Lincoln lived, struggled, and triumphed, every boy who is igno-rant, is in poverty, is despised or discouraged, holds his head a little higher. His heart beats a little faster, his ambition to do something and be something is a little stronger, because Lincoln blazed the way.[8]

Booker T. Washington, former slave and educator

The leading rule for the lawyer, as for the man of every other calling, is diligence. Leave nothing for tomorrow which can be done today.[9]

Universal idleness would speedily result in universal ruin. [10]

★ ★ ★

The result is not doubtful. We shall not fail—if we stand firm, we shall not fail. [11]

★ ★ ★

Determine that the thing can and shall be done, and then we shall find the way. [12]

★ ★ ★

Adhere to your purpose and you will soon feel as well as you ever did. On the contrary, if you falter, and give up, you will lose the power to keep any resolution, and will regret it all your life. Take the advice of a friend … and stick to your purpose. [13]

★ ★ ★

I am always for the man who wishes to work. [14]

In the log schoolhouse, which he could visit but little, he was taught only reading, writing, and elementary arithmetic. Among the people of the settlement, bush farmers, and small tradesmen, he found none of uncommon intelligence or education; but some of them had a few books, which he borrowed eagerly. … Every printed page that fell into his hands he would greedily devour, and his family and friends watched him with wonder, as an uncouth boy, after his daily work, crouched in a corner of the log cabin or outside under a tree, absorbed in a book while munching his supper of corn bread.[15]

Carl Shurtz, editor, soldier, and political leader in Lincoln's day

Work, work, work, is the main thing.[16]

★ ★ ★

I am a living witness that any one of your children may look to come here [the White House] as my father's child has.[17]

—m—

He was always calculating, always planning ahead. His ambition was a little engine that knew no rest.[18]

William Herndon

—m—

If you intend to go to work, there is no better place than right where you are.[19]

Upon the subject of education, not presuming to dictate any plan or system respecting it, I can only say that I view it as the most important subject which we as a people can be engaged in.[20]

★ ★ ★

I'll study and get ready, and then the chance will come.[21]

Mr. Lincoln ... was a terribly firm man when he set his foot down—none of us—no man nor woman could rule him after he had made up his mind.[22]

Mary Todd Lincoln

Chapter 11

HUMOR

Although Lincoln's leadership and generous heart are world renowned, many people are unaware of his tremendous wit and love of humor. Lincoln said that he cared nothing for the common vices of his day, such as drink or gambling, but he loved to tell jokes and funny stories. He considered a witty story a sort of "tonic" or medicine.

Lincoln's storytelling skills were instrumental in his political success. Stephen A. Douglas, frequent object of Lincoln's funny stories, said that every one of them "was like a whack across my back." By the time Lincoln was president, he was telling and reading humorous stories as much for his own benefit as anyone else's. He used humor to help relieve the stress and personal losses he endured while in the White House.

$\mathcal{L}$aughter [is] the joyous, beautiful, universal evergreen of life.[1]

★ ★ ★

$\mathcal{I}$t was a common notion that those who laughed heartily and often never amounted to much—never made great men. If this be the case, farewell to all my glory.[2]

★ ★ ★

$\mathcal{I}$ have heard some things from New York; and if they are true, one might well say of your party there, as a drunken fellow once said when he heard the reading of an indictment for hogstealing. The clerk read on till he got to and through the words, "did steal, take, and carry away ten boars, ten sows, ten shoats, and ten pigs," at which he exclaimed, "Well, by golly, that is the most equally divided gang of hogs I ever did hear of!" If there is any other gang of hogs more equally divided than the Democrats of New York are about this time, I have not heard of it.[3]

$\mathcal{I}$ have now come to the conclusion never again to think of marrying, and for this reason—I can never be satisfied with anyone who would be blockhead enough to have me.[4]

★   ★   ★

$\mathcal{I}$ feel like I once did when I met a woman riding horseback in the woods. As I stopped to let her pass, she also stopped, and, looking at me intently, said: "I do believe you are the ugliest man I ever saw." Said I, "Madam, you are probably right, but I can't help it!" "No," said she, "you can't help it, but you might stay at home!"[5]

★   ★   ★

$\mathcal{M}$r. Chairman, this work is exclusively the work of politicians; a set of men who have interests aside from the interests of the people, and who, to say the most of them, are, taken as a mass, at least one long step removed from honest men. I say this with the greater freedom because, being a politician myself, none can regard it as personal.[6]

Every one of his stories seems like a whack across my back. … Nothing else—not any of his arguments or any of his replies to my questions—disturbs me. But when he begins to tell a story, I feel that I am to be overmatched. [7]

Stephen A. Douglas

—✺—

I remember being once much amused at seeing two partially intoxicated men engaged in a fight with their great coats on, which fight, after a long and rather harmless contest, ended in each having fought himself out of his own coat and into that of the other. [8]

 —*Lincoln describing how the two political parties*
 had swapped positions on an issue

★ ★ ★

I was not very much accustomed to flattery, and it came the sweeter to me. I was rather like the Hoosier with the gingerbread, when he said he reckoned he loved it better than any other man, and got less of it. [9]

Others have been made fools of by the girls, but this can never with truth be said of me. I most emphatically, in this instance, made a fool of myself.[10]

$\mathcal{W}$e have all heard of the animal standing in doubt between two stacks of hay and starving to death. The like of that would never happen to General Cass. Place the stacks a thousand miles apart, he would stand stock-still midway between them, and eat them both at once, and the green grass along the line would be apt to suffer some, too.[11]

    —Lincoln was ridiculing Lewis Cass,
      the Democrats' 1848 candidate for president

★ ★ ★

$\mathcal{P}$lease have the Adjutant General ascertain whether 2nd Licut. of Co. D. 2nd Infantry—Alexander E. Drake—is not entitled to promotion. His wife thinks he is.[12]

ℋas it not got down as thin as the homeopathic soup that was made by boiling the shadow of a pigeon that had starved to death? [13]

> —*Lincoln used this analogy to describe how "thin"*
> *one of Stephen A. Douglas's political arguments was*

★ ★ ★

𝒯he opinion of Mr. Jefferson, in one branch at least, is, in the hands of Mr. Polk, like McFingal's gun—"bears wide and kicks the owner over." [14]

★ ★ ★

𝒮ending men [to General McClellan] is like shoveling fleas across a barnyard—half of them never get there. [15]

> —*Lincoln expressing frustration over McClellan's*
> *constant demand for reinforcements*

His expression in repose was sad and dull; but his ever-recurring humor, at short intervals, flashed forth with the brilliancy of an electric light. I observed but two well-defined expressions in his countenance; one, that of a pure, thoughtful, honest man, absorbed by a sense of duty and responsibility; the other, that of a humorist so full of fun that he could not keep it all in. His power of analysis was wonderful. He strengthened every case he stated, and no anecdote or joke ever lost force or effect from his telling. He invariably carried thc listener with him to the very climax, and when that was reached in relating a humorous story, he laughed all over. His large mouth assumed an unexpected and comical shape, the skin on his nose gathered into wrinkles, and his small eyes, though partly closed, emitted infectious rays of fun. It was not only the aptness of his stories, but his way of telling them, and his own unfeigned enjoyment, that gave them zest, even among the gravest men and upon the most serious occasions. [16]

James B. Fry, U.S. provost marshal-general during the Lincoln administration

$\mathcal{D}$ear Sir: Says Tom to John, "Here's your old rotten wheelbarrow. I've broke it, usin' on it. I wish you would mend it, case I shall want to borrow it this arter-noon." [17]

  —*Lincoln telling a joke to communicate*
  that he needed a new railroad pass

★ ★ ★

$\mathcal{T}$his he [Stephen A. Douglas] cannot deny; and so he remembers to forget it. [18]

Chapter 12

HOPE

Lincoln held that America offered mankind the greatest hope for the future. He believed several factors contributed to this great hope. American people, he believed, were so resourceful that they were unconquerable by anyone but themselves. America's natural resources were so vast that they represented the "choicest bounties of heaven." American government, in proposing equal opportunity for all, was the best yet formed by man. Finally, he believed that America would be forever blessed by God if her people would continue to seek His will and do what is "right."

It was because of his great confidence in what America could do for mankind that he considered it essential he and his generation make whatever sacrifices were necessary in order to preserve the "last, best hope of earth."

$\mathcal{L}$et us readopt the Declaration of Independence, and with it the practices and policy which harmonize with it. Let North and South—let all Americans—let all lovers of liberty everywhere join in the great and good work. If we do this, we shall not only have saved the Union, but we shall have so saved it as to make and to keep it forever worthy of the saving. We shall have so saved it that the succeeding millions of free happy people, the world over, shall rise up and call us blessed to the latest generations. [1]

★ ★ ★

$\mathcal{L}$et us be quite sober. Let us diligently apply the means, never doubting that a just God, in his own good time, will give us the rightful result. [2]

We proposed to give all a chance; and we expect the weak to grow stronger, the ignorant, wiser, and all better, and happier together.[3]

★ ★ ★

But this government must be preserved in spite of the acts of any man or set of men. It is worthy of your every effort. Nowhere in the world is presented a government of so much liberty and equality. To the humblest and poorest amongst us are held out the highest privileges and positions. The present moment finds me at the White House, yet there is as good a chance for your children as there was for my father's.[4]

★ ★ ★

It is difficult to make a man miserable when he feels worthy of himself and claims kindred to the great God who made him.[5]

$\mathcal{F}$ellow-citizens, we cannot escape history. We of this Congress and this administration will be remembered in spite of ourselves. No personal significance or insignificance can spare one or another of us. The fiery trial through which we pass will light us down, in honor or dishonor, to the latest generation. We say we are for the Union. The world will not forget that we say this. We know how to save the Union. The world knows we do know how to save it. We—even we here—hold the power and bear the responsibility. In giving freedom to the slave, we assure freedom to the free—honorable alike in what we give and what we preserve. We shall nobly save or meanly lose the last, best hope of earth. Other means may succeed; this could not fail. The way is plain, peaceful, generous, just—a way which, if followed, the world will forever applaud, and God must forever bless.[6]

The struggle
of today
is not
altogether
for today—
it is for a vast
future also.[7]

$\mathcal{Y}$et, under all circumstances, trusting to our Maker, and through His wisdom and beneficence, to the great body of our people, we will not despair, or despond.[8]

★ ★ ★

$\mathcal{W}$ith malice toward none; with charity for all; with firmness in the right, as God gives us to see the right, let us strive on to finish the work we are in: to bind up the nation's wounds; to care for him who shall have borne the battle, and for his widow, and his orphan—to do all which may achieve and cherish a just and lasting peace among ourselves, and with all nations.[9]

★ ★ ★

$\mathcal{T}$he power of hope upon the human exertion and happiness is wonderful.[10]

He saw clearly that the same high qualities, the same courage, and willingness for self-sacrifice, and devotion to the right as it was given them to see the right, belonged both to the men of the North and to the men of the South. As the years roll by, and as all of us, wherever we dwell, grow to feel an equal pride in the valor and self-devotion, alike of the men who wore the blue and the men who wore the gray, so this whole nation will grow to feel a peculiar sense of pride in the man whose blood was shed for the union of his people and for the freedom of a race; the lover of his country and all mankind; the mightiest of the mighty men who mastered the mighty days: Abraham Lincoln. [11]

Theodore Roosevelt, twenty-sixth U.S. president

By the same token that Lincoln made America free, he pushed back the boundaries of freedom everywhere, gave the spirit of liberty a wider influence throughout the world, and reestablished the dignity of man as man. [12]

Booker T. Washington

We thereby restore the national faith, the national confidence, the national feeling of brotherhood. We thereby reinstate the spirit of concession and compromise—that spirit which has never failed us in past perils, and which may be safely trusted for all the future. [13]

★ ★ ★

I wish you a long life and prosperity individually, and pray that with the perpetuity of those institutions under which we have all so long lived and prospered, our happiness may be secured, our future made brilliant, and the glorious destiny of our country established forever. [14]

126

We are a great empire. We are eighty years old. We stand at once the wonder and admiration of the whole world, and we must enquire what it is that has given us so much prosperity, and we shall understand that to give up that one thing, would be to give up all future prosperity. This cause is that every man can make himself. It has been said that such a race of prosperity has been run nowhere else. [15]

★ ★ ★

I have often inquired of myself, what great principle or idea it was that kept this Confederacy so long together. It was not the mere matter of the separation of the colonies from the mother land; but something in that Declaration giving liberty, not alone to the people of this country, but hope to the world for all future time. It was that which gave promise that in due time the weights should be lifted from the shoulders of all men, and that all should have an equal chance. [16]

The Gettysburg Address

Fourscore and seven years ago our fathers brought forth on this continent a new nation, conceived in liberty, and dedicated to the proposition that all men are created equal.

Now we are engaged in a great civil war, testing whether that nation, or any nation so conceived and so dedicated, can long endure. We are met on a great battlefield of that war. We have come to dedicate a portion of that field as a final resting place for those who here gave their lives that that nation might live. It is altogether fitting and proper that we should do this.

But, in a larger sense, we cannot dedicate—we cannot consecrate—we cannot hallow—this ground. The brave men, living and dead, who struggled here, have consecrated it far above our poor power to add or detract. The world will little note nor long remember what we say here, but it can never forget what they did here. It is for us, the living, rather, to be dedicated here to the unfinished work which they who fought here have thus far so nobly advanced. It is rather for us to be here dedicated to the great task remaining before us—that from these honored dead we take increased devotion to that cause for which they gave the last full measure of devotion; that we here highly resolve that these dead shall not have died in vain; that this nation, under God, shall have a new birth of freedom; and that government of the people, by the people, for the people, shall not perish from the earth.[1]

Lincoln's
Second Inaugural Address

At this second appearing to take the oath of the presidential office, there is less occasion for an extended address than there was at the first. Then a statement, somewhat in detail, of a course to be pursued, seemed fitting and proper. Now, at the expiration of four years, during which public declarations have been constantly called forth on every point and phase of the great contest which still absorbs the attention, and engrosses the energies [*sic*] of the nation, little that is new could be presented. The progress of our arms, upon which all else chiefly depends, is as well known to the public as to myself; and it is, I trust, reasonably satisfactory and encouraging to all. With high hope for the future, no prediction in regard to it is ventured.

On the occasion corresponding to this four years ago, all thoughts were anxiously directed to an impending civil-war. All dreaded it—all sought to avert it. While the inaugural address was being delivered from this place, devoted altogether to saving the Union without war, insurgent agents were in the city seeking to destroy it without war—seeking to dissolve the Union, and divide effects, by negotiation. Both parties deprecated war; but one of them would make war rather than let the nation survive; and the other would accept war rather than let it perish. And the war came.

One eighth of the whole population were colored slaves, not distributed generally over the Union, but localized in the Southern part of it. These slaves constituted a peculiar and powerful interest. All knew that this interest was, somehow, the cause of the war. To strengthen, perpetuate, and extend this interest was the object for which the insurgents would rend the Union, even by war; while the government claimed no right to do more than to restrict the territorial enlargement of it. Neither party expected for the war, the magnitude, or the duration, which it has already attained. Neither anticipated that the cause of the conflict might cease with, or even before, the conflict itself should cease. Each looked for an easier triumph, and a result less fundamental and astounding. Both read the same Bible, and pray to the same God; and each invokes His aid against the other. It may seem strange that any men should dare to ask a just God's assistance in wringing their bread from the sweat of other men's faces; but let us judge not that we be not judged. The prayers of both could not be answered; that of neither has been answered fully. The Almighty has His own purposes. "Woe unto the world because of offences! for it must needs be that offences come; but woe to that man by whom the offence cometh!" If we shall suppose that American Slavery is one of those offences which, in the providence of God, must needs come, but which, having continued through His appointed time, He now wills to remove, and that He gives to both North and South, this terrible war, as the woe due to those by whom the offence came, shall we discern therein any departure from those divine attributes which the believers in a Living God always ascribe to Him? Fondly do we hope—fervently do we pray— that this mighty scourge of war may speedily pass away. Yet, if God wills that it continue, until all the wealth piled by the bond-man's two hundred and fifty years of unrequited toil shall be sunk, and until every drop of blood drawn with the lash, shall be paid by another drawn with the sword, as was said three thousand years ago, so still it must be said "the judgments of the Lord, are true and righteous altogether."

With malice toward none; with charity for all; with firmness in the right, as God gives us to see the right, let us strive on to finish the work we are in; to bind up the nation's wounds; to care for him who shall have borne the battle, and for his widow, and his orphan—to do all which may achieve and cherish a just, and a lasting peace, among ourselves, and with all nations.[1]

Acknowledgments

I am thankful for the kind assistance and encouragement provided by many people during my preparation of this book. At the Library of Congress, my good friend Clark Evans, the senior reference librarian of the Rare Book and Special Collections Reading Room, was very helpful with many of the references as well as providing access to rare Lincoln materials. John Sellers, Lincoln curator at the Library of Congress, provided valuable guidance during my efforts to identify the source of some hard-to-find Lincoln quotes. Jennifer Brathovde and Maja Keech of the Prints and Photographs Reading Room provided guidance in finding Lincoln photos.

Tom Schwartz of the Abraham Lincoln Association in Springfield, Illinois, provided invaluable help when I was tracking down some hard-to-identify Lincoln quotes.

Special thanks to Professor Michael Burlingame of Connecticut College, Tom Schwartz of the Abraham Lincoln Association, and Ed Bearss, chief historian emeritus of the National Park Service, for patiently reviewing and commenting on the manuscript. Even then, I accept full responsibility for the contents of this book.

I also thank Woody West, editor of the *Washington Times*'s "Civil War Page" for giving me my first break in publishing, and my friends Stan Kandebo, of *Aviation Week* magazine, and Dick Dykeman for offering helpful suggestions and encouragement in my various writing efforts along the way.

I would like to thank various family members. These include my wife, Jean, who not only provided invaluable advice and encouragement but who also helped with the proofreading and put up with my interminable Lincoln stories. I also want to thank my father, Harold Leidner of Greenville, Illinois; and my "good ol' father-in-law," Buddy Norris of Bryantown, Maryland. Both provided constant encouragement and support in my various writing projects.

Finally, I would like to thank my editor, Mike Towle. Without his vision, patience, and skill, this book would have never happened.

Notes

Chapter 1: Leadership

1. Nicolay, John G., and John Hay, editors, *Complete Works of Lincoln* (*hereafter nh*) (New York: Francis D. Tandy, 1905); v. 10, 65; 4.4.64.

2. Burlingame, Michael, *An Oral History of Abraham Lincoln: John G. Nicolay's Interviews and Essays* (Carbondale: Southern Illinois University Press, 1996), 54-55.

3. Pratt, Harry E., *Concerning Mr. Lincoln* (Springfield, Illinois: Abraham Lincoln Association, 1944), 52.

4. nh, v. 6, 184-185; 3.4.61.

5. nh, v. 5, 327-328; 2.27.60.

6. Herndon, William H., and Jesse W. Weik, *Herndon's Lincoln: The True Story of a Great Life* (Chicago: Belford, Clarke, and Co., 1889), 537.

7. Basler, Roy P., *Collected Works of Abraham Lincoln* (*hereafter Basler*) (New Brunswick, New Jersey: Rutgers University Press, 1953) v. 2, 547; 8.17.58.

8. nh, v. 7, 52; 12.3.61.

9. nh, v. 10, 68; 4.4.64.

10. Basler, v. 4, 149; 12.10.60.

11. nh, v. 10, 66; 4.4.64.

12. Rice, Allen T., *Reminiscences of Abraham Lincoln by Distinguished Men of His Time* (New York: North American Review, 1888), 577.

13. Rice, 493.

14. nh, v. 1, 46; 1.2.37.

15. Carpenter, F. B., *The Inner Life of Abraham Lincoln* (Boston: Houghton, Mifflin & Co., 1883), 258-259 [quote attributed to Lincoln]*.

16. Rice, 365.

*—Quotes that are generally accepted by scholars as having originated with Lincoln, but which have no written backup in Lincoln's handwriting, are listed as "quotes attributed to Lincoln" in the endnotes.

Chapter 2: Honesty

1. Herndon, 606.

2. nh, v. 3, 170; 7.17.58.

3. nh, v. 4, 113; 9.18.58.

4. nh, v. 1, 89; 4.1.38.

5. nh, v. 2, 143; 7.1.50.

6. Thomas, Benjamin, *Abraham Lincoln*

(New York: Alfred Knopf, 1952), 182.

7. nh, v. 2, 28; 6.20.48.

8. nh, v. 4, 190-191; 9.18.58.

9. nh, v. 4, 376; 10.13.58.

10. nh, v. 4, 51; 7.15.58.

11. Turner, J., and L. Turner, *Mary Todd Lincoln: Her Life and Letters* (New York: Alfred A. Knopf, 1972), 180.

12. Herndon, 400 [quote attributed to Lincoln].

13. nh, v. 2, 243; 10.16.54.

14. Burlingame, 1996, 96.

15. nh, v. 3, 336; 8.27.58.

16. Herndon, 346 [quote attributed to Lincoln].

17. Wilson, Douglas, and Rodney Davis, editors, *Herndon's Informants: Letters, Interviews, and Statements About Abraham Lincoln* (Urbana, Illinois: University of Illinois Press, 1998), 386.

18. nh, v. 10, 158; 7.4.64.

19. Hertz, Emanuel, *Abraham Lincoln: A New Portrait* (New York: Liveright, 1931), v. 2, 530; 2.8.42.

20. Rothschild, Alonzo, *Honest Abe: A Study in Integrity Based on the Early Life of Abraham Lincoln* (New York: Houghton-Mifflin, 1917), 64.

21. Rice, 575.

CHAPTER 3: FAITH

1. nh, v. 8, 33, 9.13.62.

2. nh, v. 8, 52-53; 9.30.62.

3. nh, v. 10, 7.7.64, 149.

4. Basler, v. 6, 536;10.24.63.

5. Carpenter, 282 [quote attributed to Lincoln].

6. Basler, v. 3, 204.

7. Herndon, 538.

8. nh, v. 8, 50-51; 10.26.62.

9. nh, v. 2, 280-281; 8.15.55.

10. nh, v. 10, 215-216; 9.4.64.

11. Carpenter, 188 [quote attributed to Lincoln].

12. nh, v. 8, 174, 1.5.63.

13. Herndon, p. 359.

14. nh, v. 8, 235-237; 3.30.63 [quote was probably co-authored by the secretary of state].

15. Speed, Joshua, *Reminiscences of Abraham Lincoln and Notes of a Visit to California* (Louisville, Kentucky: John P.

Morgan and Company, 1884), 32-33
[quote attributed to Lincoln].

16. nh, 10, 218; 9.7.64.

17. nh, v. 6, 110-111; 2.11.61.

CHAPTER 4: THE PEOPLE

1. Hertz, 1931, v. 2, 793; 11.21.60
[quote attributed to Lincoln].

2. nh, v. 6, 312; 7.4.61.

3. nh, v. 6, 183; 3.4.61.

4. nh, v. 6, 112; 2.11.61.

5. nh, v. 1, 36-37; 1.27.38.

6. nh, v. 6, 321; 7.4.61.

7. Wilson, 182.

8. nh, v. 6, 130; 2.15.61.

9. nh, v. 2, 69; 7.27.48.

10. nh, v. 7, 30; 12.3.61.

11. nh, v. 6, 184, 3.4.61.

12. nh, v. 6, 143; 2.19.61.

13. Wilson, 592.

14. nh, v. 6, 121; 2.13.61.

15. Hertz, 1931, v. 2, 806; 2.11.61
[quote attributed to Lincoln].

16. nh, v. 6, 134; 2.16.61.

17. Hertz, 1931, v. 2, 805; 2.11.61
[quote attributed to Lincoln].

18. nh, v. 6, 123; 2.14.61.

19. nh, v. 1, 26; 1.11.37.

20. Braden, Waldo, editor, *Building the Myth: Selected Speeches Memorializing Abraham Lincoln* (*hereafter Braden*) (Urbana, Illinois: University of Illinois Press, 1990), 101-102.

21. nh, v. 5, 232; 9.17.59.

22. nh, v. 8, 157, 12.31.62.

23. Angle, Paul, *Abraham Lincoln by Some Men Who Knew Him* (Chicago: Americana House Publishers, 1950), 24-25.

CHAPTER 5: KINDNESS

1. nh, v. 7, 293; 7.26.62.

2. nh, v. 7, 298; 7.28.62.

3. nh, v. 7, 303; 8.4.62.

4. Rice, 338-339.

5. Carpenter, 203.

6. nh, v. 10, 263-264; 11.10.64.

7. Speed, 1884, 39 [quote attributed to Lincoln].

8. nh, v. 6, 185; 3.4.61.

9. nh, v. 9, 303; 2.5.64.

10. nh, v. 11, IX.

11. Hertz, Emanuel, *The Hidden Lincoln, From the Letters and Papers of William H. Herndon* (New York: Viking Press, 1938), 327 [quote attributed to Lincoln].

12. Herndon, 535.

13. nh, v. 6, 72; 11.20.60.

14. nh, v. 10, 262; 11.8.64.

15. Lamon, Dorothy, editor, *Recollections of Abraham Lincoln 1847–1865 by Ward Hill Lamon* (Chicago: A. C. McClurg and Co., 1895), 87 [quote attributed to Lincoln].

16. Rice, 338.

CHAPTER 6: LIBERTY

1. nh, v. 5, 94; 11.19.58.

2. Basler, v. 3, 327.

3. nh, v. 5, 126; 4.6.59.

4. nh, v. 11, 110; 9.11.58 .

5. nh, v. 10, 77; 4.18.64.

6. nh, v. 5, 61; 10.15.58.

7. Rice, 193-195.

8. Basler, v. 4, 169; Jan 61.

9. nh, v. 1, 49-50; 1.27.38.

10. nh, v. 3, 51; 7.10.58.

11. nh, v. 5, 361; 3.6.60.

12. nh 1, 36; 1.27.37.

13. nh, v. 2, 287; 8.24.55.

14. Braden, 99.

15. nh, v. 2, 184; 7.1.54.

16. nh, v. 5, 65.

17. nh, v. 1, 42-43; 1.27.38.

18. Rice, 210.

19. nh, v. 9, xiv.

CHAPTER 7: COMMON SENSE

1. Basler, v. 4, 184; 2.4.61.

2. nh, v. 5, 190; 9.17.59.

3. nh, v. 11, 54; 3.15.65.

4. Dennett, Tyler, editor, *Lincoln and the Civil War in the Diaries and Letters of John Hay* (New York: Dodd, Meade, and Company, 1939) 143; 12.23.63.

5. Basler, v. 6, 538; 10.26.63.

6. Carpenter, 312-313.

7. nh, v.1, 2; 3.9.32.

8. nh, v. 2,125; 7.13.49.

9. nh, v. 7, 245; 6.30.62.

10. Rice, 427.

11. Nicolay, John G., and John Hay, *Abraham Lincoln: A History* (New York: The Century Co., 1904), v. 10, 377.

12. nh, v. 2, 142.

13. nh, v. 1,197; 2.22.42.

14. nh, v. 11, 87; 4.11.65.

15. Braden, 142.

16. Basler, v. 2, 437; 4.6.58.

17. nh, v. 6, 184.

18. Rice, 427-428.

19. Basler, v. 4, 270; 3.4.61.

20. Braden, 98.

21. Hertz, 1938, 406 [quote attributed to Lincoln].

22. nh, v. 11, 85; 4.11.65.

CHAPTER 8: CHARACTER

1. Fehrenbacher, Don, and Virginia Fehrenbacher, editors, *Recollected Words of Abraham Lincoln* (Stanford, California: Stanford University Press, 1996), 43 [quote attributed to Lincoln].

2. nh, v. 2, 192; 10.16.54.

3. Basler, v. 7, 383; 6.9.64.

4. nh, v. 9, 199; 11.2.63.

5. Basler, v. 7, 507, 8.19.64.

6. nh, v. 1, 56; 8.16.37.

7. Wilson, 499.

8. nh, v. 1, 137; 12.20.39.

9. nh, v. 8, 69; 10.27.62.

10. Rice, 575-576.

11. Basler, v. 3, 436; 9.16.59.

12. Herndon, 531 [quote attributed to Lincoln].

13. Braden, 118.

14. Burlingame, Michael (editor) *Lincoln Observed: The Civil War Dispatches of Noah Brooks* (Baltimore: The Johns Hopkins University Press, 1998 [quote attributed to Lincoln].

15. nh, v. 7, 304; 8.6.62.

16. Sandburg, Carl, *Abraham Lincoln: The War Years* (New York: Charles Scribner's Sons, 1939), v. 3, 559 [quote attributed to Lincoln].

17. nh, v. 1, 53; 5.7.37.

18. nh, v. 11,92; 4.11.65.

19. nh, v. 5, XXIX.

20. nh, v. 7, 159.

CHAPTER 9: DEMOCRACY

1. Basler, v. 2, 385; 12.10.56.

2. nh, v. 6, 157; 2.22.61.

3. nh, v. 2, 184; 7.1.54.

4. nh v. 6, 151-152; 2.21.61.

5. Basler, v. 2, 532; 8.1.58.

6. nh, v. 2, 186-187; 7.1.54.

7. nh, v. 5, IX.

8. nh, v. 3, 252; 8.21.58.

9. nh, v. 2, 226-227; 10.16.54.

10. Dennett, 19-20.

11. Braden, 101-102.

12. nh, v. 1, 14; 6.13.36.

13. nh, v. 6, 304; 7.4.61.

14. nh, v. 2, 165; 7.6.52.

15. nh, v. 2, 37; 6.20.48.

16. nh, v. 2, 235; 10.16.54.

17. nh, v. 1, 42; 1.27.38.

18. nh, v. 4, 226; 12.28.57.

19. Basler, v. 4, 197; 2.12.61.

CHAPTER 10: PERSEVERANCE

1. Basler, v. 2, 327; 11.5.55.

2. Basler, v. 4, 87; 7.22.60.

3. Basler, v. 3, 90; 9.6.58.

4. nh, v. 7, 240; 6.29.62.

5. Wilson, 113.

6. nh, v. 1, 138; 12.26.39.

7. nh, v. 2, 57; 7.10.48.

8. Braden, 155.

9. nh, v. 2, 46; 6.20.48.

10. nh, 1, 314; 12.1.47.

11. nh, v. 3, 15; 6.16.58.

12. Basler, v. 1, 489; 7.20.48.

13. Basler, v. 5, 288; 6.28.62.

14. Basler, v. 7, 495; 8.15.64.

15. Krans, H. S., *The Lincoln Tribute Book* (New York: G. P. Putnam's Sons, 1909), 22.

16. nh, v. 6, 59; 9.25.60.

17. nh, v. 10, 202-203; 8.22.64.

18. Herndon, 375.

19. nh, v. 2, 150; 11.4.51.

20. nh, v. 1, 7; 3.9.32.

21. Tarbell, Ida M., and J. M. Davis, *The Early Life of Abraham Lincoln* (New York: McClure, 1896), 62 [quote attributed to Lincoln].

22. Wilson, 360.

CHAPTER 11: HUMOR

1. Fehrenbacher, 340 [quote attributed to Lincoln].

2. Herndon, William H., "An Analysis of the Character of Abraham Lincoln," *Abraham Lincoln Quarterly*, I (1940–41), 420 [quote attributed to Lincoln].

3. nh, v. 2, 88; 7.27.48.

4. nh, v. 1, 92; 4.1.38.

5. Angle, 51.

6. nh, v. 1, 27; 1.11.37.

7. Zall, P. M., editor, *Abe Lincoln Laughing* (Berkeley, California: University of California Press, 1982), 5.

8. nh, v. 5, 125; 4.6.59.

9. Zall, 19.

10. nh, v. 1, 92; 4.1.38.

11. nh, v. 2, 83; 7.27.48.

12. Basler, v. 5, 22; 11.13.61.

13. Basler, v. 3, 279; 10.13.58.

14. Basler, v. 1, 485; 6.20.48.

15. Hertz, Emanuel, *Lincoln Talks* (New York: Viking, 1939), 459 [quote attributed to Lincoln].

16. Rice, 388.

17. Basler, v. 2, 330; 2.13.56.

18. Basler, v. 2, 552; 8.21.58.

CHAPTER 12: HOPE

1. nh, v. 2, 248; 10.16.54.

2. nh, v. 9, 102; 5.26.63.

3. nh, v. 2, 184; 7.1.54.

4. nh, v. 10, 209; 8.31.64.

5. nh, v. 8, 5; 8.14.62.

6. nh, v. 8, 131; 12.1.62.

7. nh, v. 7, 60; 12.3.61.

8. Basler, v. 2, 89; 7.25.50.

9. nh, v. 2, 47; 3.4.65.

10. nh, v. 2, 185; 7.1.54.

11. Braden, 167.

12. Braden, 154.

13. nh, v. 2, 241; 10.16.54.

14. nh, v. 6, 136; 2.16.61.

15. Basler v. 2, p. 364; 8.27.56.

16. nh, v. 6, 157; 2.22.61.

THE GETTYSBURG ADDRESS

1. nh, v. 9, 209-210.

LINCOLN'S SECOND INAUGURAL ADDRESS

1. nh, v. 2, 44–47; 3.4.65.

The photograph on the title page and the chapter openers is from *A Witness to an Era* by D. Mark Katz where it was reproduced from the collection of Lloyd Ostendorf.

Page 17. From the Library of Congress
Page 27. From the Library of Congress
Page 31. From the Library of Congress
Page 39. From the Library of Congress
Page 41. From the Library of Congress
Page 47. From the Library of Congress
Page 59. From the Library of Congress
Page 61. From the collection of D. Mark Katz

Page 67. From the Library of Congress
Page 77. From the Library of Congress
Page 85. From the Library of Congress
Page 95. From the Library of Congress
Page 103. From the Library of Congress
Page 113. From the Library of Congress
Page 122. From the National Archives